Note for Librarians: a cataloguing record for this book that includes Dewey Decimal Classification and US Library of Congress numbers is available from the National Library of Canada. The complete cataloguing record can be obtained from the National Library's online database at: www.nlc-bnc.ca/amicus/index-e.html
ISBN 1-4120-3642-9

TRAFFORD

Offices in Canada, USA, Ireland, UK and Spain
This book was published *on-demand* in cooperation with Trafford Publishing. On-demand publishing is a unique process and service of making a book available for retail sale to the public taking advantage of on-demand manufacturing and Internet marketing. On-demand publishing includes promotions, retail sales, manufacturing, order fulfilment, accounting and collecting royalties on behalf of the author.

Book sales in Europe:
Trafford Publishing (UK) Ltd., Enterprise House, Wistaston Road Business Centre, Wistaston Road, Crewe CW2 7RP UNITED KINGDOM
phone 01270 251 396 (local rate 0845 230 9601)
facsimile 01270 254 983; info.uk@trafford.com

Book sales for North America and international:
Trafford Publishing, 6E–2333 Government St.,
Victoria, BC V8T 4P4 CANADA
phone 250 383 6864 (toll-free 1 888 232 4444)
fax 250 383 6804; email to bookstore@trafford.com

www.trafford.com/robots/04-1470.html

10 9 8 7 6 5 4 3 2

The Bird Man and His Shadow

Cover artwork based on a Navajo sand painting of the Bird Man (Front) and from a symbol the author received during his vision quest in Arizona and New Mexico in 1993. (Back)
by Kevin H. Quannie, Hopi artist
of Kykotsmovi Village, Arizona
www.kevinhoracequannie.com

Author's photo by Peggy Mesler

Artwork arranged and contents edited by
Ferenc Katona Budapest, Hungary
www.alitera.hu

PAUL KATONA

THE BIRD MAN AND HIS SHADOW

SAN LOUIS OBISPO
2004

A TRUE POEM
IS NOT LIKE PLAYING GOLF ON THE TURF
OF A PRESTIGIOUS COUNTRY CLUB,

BUT SOOTHSAYING
FROM THE GUTS
OF A SACRIFICIAL ANIMAL.

Lawrence Durrell

Prologue
by the author

To love unconditionally, you need the enormity of the divine, or at second best, a true devotion to mankind. I believe that in a hidden chamber of our hearts, or in an unexplored segment of our unconscious, we all have a pure element which calls for the ultimate truth and love experience, even if that experience can never be attained in its entirety.

The title of this volume, the Bird Man (an approximate and distant Native American version of our very own Jesus Christ), was chosen because of the dual nature of Man. In this context the Bird Man represents our higher, divine self - what the Hindus call the "Atman".

A Lakota elder once purported that on this Earth there are two of everything. Thus to achieve a balance of forces we have a light side as well as dark side (the Shadow), and we spend a great deal of time trying to understand these opposing forces. The Shadow hides in the unconscious, but it is well represented in our conscious mind through its earthly ally, called the Ego. To conquer the Shadow is essential to our existence and the fulfillment of our destiny. This battle is a work of a lifetime and in certain cases, the work of many lifetimes. The Shadow can not be destroyed, for that would be self-mutilation. Our only remaining alternative is to transform it through self-redemption. In essence, this lies at the heart of every human life, whether the transmutation executed or not. To lessen the burden of this task, some, if not all of us, at one time or other, individually or collectively, will project our own Shadow onto others. This then results in unjustified guilt-complexes, witchunts, and on a larger scale, genocide and war.

When I am out of harmony with the physical world, it rolls me over like a ton of rocks. When I am illuminated, I can see the Creator in the bend of a grass blade, and in things and people who reveal themselves to me during such moments. These fluctuations of the soul what I am about to share with you now. Most of my poems have been conceived under these conditions, from all over the spectrum - the inner and outer Universe that is. Even though on occasions they touch the sky, do not expect too much from them for they exist to resonate of what is already in you.

Feel the pain, it purifies. Fly with the imagination: it sets you free. Remember: everything is created by love, or by the lack of it. Do not blame: transcend and revive.

A task of a lifetime, or the fulfillment of a single moment: go with it.

Love, live and marvel at the stars!

Best of journey,

Paul Katona

Contents

After the Act

The physical recall
seems biblical
but for me
it is rather
personal

temptations
nearly destroyed
me

yet as
a wild mustang
shed the saddle
so I
despise
the word:

sin

the force
reinforced me
in my ambiguous ways

now
I can not
wait to be
ancient and wise
gracefully
smiling at the flesh

and
love as
Gandhi did

if I can

Antagonism

Master of
slaves

slaves led
master

me and my
senses

(Who's who?)

Apocalypse

when
the Sun retreated
and the bombing
temporarily stopped
the birds became silent
then
the Father Sky spoke:
collaborate no more!
Call the Snake
by its unspeakable
name!

I said:
It's too late!
The Serpent already
circumvented
the Globe!

The Archers
of dark forces
were unleashed as
written by
the Prophets

Time is
pregnant with
the bastard child
of the Fallen Angel
whilst
corporations
making their
profits
as
pigs being
dissected
mothers shot to death
nations turned into
mere masses

as I am,
leaving all behind
starting to climb the last refuge:
my inner Mount Everest

to become a
frozen, sacred
snow leopard

A Streetcar Named Desire
(the farmer's wife)

When she was
full of life
decadent and artistic
as the gods meant it
she played
a passionate wife
in an American
classic

As time passed
she embarked
on an another
streetcar called
Destiny
married a local
Kowalski with
a tractor's key and
chewing tobacco
in his pocket
and a Blue Jay cap
on his balding head
hopelessly lacking
the understanding
of foreplay
and passion

now,
having a family
she's too tired
to walk away

In Indian summer
on a late afternoon
she stares through
the falling leafs' contours
against the blessed rays
of the dying Sun

washing
the same set of dishes
for the last fifteen years

Avenue Of Broken Dreams Accepted

All the mornings
alienate

Oh, this man from the
rising Sun's house

like an Arab, with shiny headdress
and sunglasses
a real personality test

Sitting in a LUCKY cart,
Happy day!
With a healthy smile
this fellow says
an another dweller of
planet St. Julien*
a truly
blessed man

A pink plastic chair
(like a baby monkey)
being carried on
the shoulder of my favorite
black man
of the premises
must be his
talisman, or the
last remembrance of a
distant past, blurred
but not forgotten

approaching
Raincoat and Beard
(The lost Russian poet)
the way I call him:
a strange, but cosmic friend

He talks incessantly
to the thin air
his eyes, like
a true writer's
always creating

I mourn me in him.

And there's the Pig!
He knows.

Lying on the sidewalk
with his big belly,
not returning my
unspoken, but
enthusiastic
Lazarus-greeting
(Rise!)

Staring with an animal's
ignorant, but
defiant eyes
(no doubt: he would eat me
in lack of his daily burger)
I am not sure
but suspecting:
he urinates with his pants on

Oh, my distant,
dirty, unloved brothers
from the family
of Man

I wonder
if we,
with our cars
bank accounts and
delusions of a secured life
are really more
than you?

** St. Julien street is a part of Skid Row
in downtown Los Angeles*

Awe

Ah, the eyes,
the human eyes!

Vast oceans and
universes
and a world of
cosmic distances
within the flesh

What a divine,
terribly tragic
hopeless
all-promising
predetermined
situation that is:

the Holy Grail
in a bootlegger's
decaying cabin!

Brain on the sidewalk

(a man was shot to death)

The bang was
a big bang

scream, or rather
an upset murmur
ensued among
the homeless

What made me
to go and see the body?

To check my nerves perhaps
or else the twisted curiosity
of the living over
the dead

God be with his soul!
said this shaken black brother
right next to me
exactly, what I thought
yet a woman nearby
hysterically exclaimed
Look! His head is moving!
He's not dead!

but the air,
contaminated
with death
slowly settled
on our shoulders and
consciousness

Nothing new,
but still, the men of duty
were nervous as arrived
what a nonsense,
I thought, since the universal act
was irreversibly done

and a white sheet
was thrown over
the body

Budapest, 1956

In memoriam of the Hungarian
Freedom Fighter

T-34
was the type of
battle tank
the Russkies used
in WW II.
and against
teenagers with stones
in November,
Nineteen Fifty-Six

on the streets
of the Paris of the East
Budapest

Do it! Do it!
We will support you!
Was the exuberant
announcement
on the Radio
Voice of America
but
when it all began
the Champion of Democracy
(perhaps motivated
by oil only)
just stood by,
unmoved

and
the Man of the Year in 1956
by the Time Magazine
was the Hungarian Freedom Fighter

from the Paris of The East
Budapest

Who,
by this time
was betrayed,
murdered and
laid to rest

The Juveniles
were executed
by the Regime
a year or so later
a day after their
eighteenth birthday
in keeping with
Geneva Paper

Their death note
was a telegram
by the
State Department
about observing
Holy Status Quo,
during and after
this whole
inconvenient,
annoying and
rebellious
Hungarian
incident

sent
(via Tito,
the Yugoslav
partisan-hero)

to the bloody handed
not-so
pro-democracy
gatekeepers
of the
Iron Curtain

in Moscow

and in the Paris of the East
Budapest

Dear me

Repent!
Said I
Me listened
not

I swear
I saw the
Devil
and a bunch
of demons
behind
the Cross

Oh dear,
what to me
now?

December 9

Like unconscious,
rude and massive
dark rocks
these days
fell upon me

What was my sin?
Offended who,
when, why
who am I?

Did I kill
innocents
(perhaps
in an another realm)
by simply
lifting my wineglass ?

I stand before
my own terrible
mystery, trembling,
dirty, abandoned
by higher powers

questioning
the sense of it all,
I collect myself

again

Declaration of Independence
(me and you)

I am on guard

I must
love and
protect me
against
the unconscious
cannibal
animal
hiding
in you

I am a dreamer

I will
not dream
instead, but
for you
too

I am a man

I will live
and die
by myself
but will not lead
or follow
you

I am a citizen

I will not vote
against
or for
you

I am
who I am

a Child of the Universe
bound not
by government,
party doctrines
the Church
or by
you

Déjà vu

Hundreds of
pawn soldiers' blood
unseen
seeps through the screen
of CNN

We all guilty and soaked
we all said "Barabbas"
though nobody asked

The President-King
declared all this
honorable death

What is honor?

Oil and vinegar
on your table
the neighbor's blood
on your knife

Circus, bread
Hollywood paper-gladiators
idols and pseudo-romances
are the need of the
masses

supplied by
(What a meritorious charity!)

the Establishment
and its little bulldog on leash,
the media
waging its tail happily

Have anything changed
since Roman vanity?

Dilemma of an Angel
(en route to the womb)

Ah!
the aura
of this planet
emanates to light years
tells it all!
The straightforwardness
of the heart is a scarcity
in this
gravitational reality

Everything is
so disgustingly
physical!
Hidden daggers
in words and smiles,
sweet poison
blood, tears
pseudo-progress
deception of the self
and others
then Death

The thought
of becoming human is
so Hollywoodishly
scary

Perhaps it is
a blessing or
heavenly bad luck,
but this phase
must be done
if I want
to promote
on St. Peter's Corporate
Ladder to Eternity

or else
by Divine decree
for the
love of mankind
and for its
questionable
Destiny

Epilogue to a Lover

Your heart

sending erotically
polarized blood
through your
pulsating throat
gasping for air
in the saddle
of pleasure
endowing your
graces on a
stranger

still
remembers me.

now
I cry for
not hearing you
in the cavalcade
of tempting voices

Dead, white orchids
are
my past words
and regrets

Our
lifeless love
unmourned
lies in a
sorrow-wood casket

Our names are
written with colorless chalk
on the blackboard of
lovers
clinically dead

Our embracing,
defenseless smiles
not to be harmed
by the softly falling
clods of the

ever loving
Earth

Eternal

Why white,
white dolomite
her virginity is

when

on exalted nights
as manhood
awakened
with divine energy
the chosen man
cries in agony

knowing

she missed the
cosmic rendezvous
again, just to
disperse her
redemptive graces
to the ordinary

How can
the female be
so Mary-like and
simultaneously
so unholy?

Etruscan Love

Mahogany marble
round and rising
a die-for fountain
of life and orgasms
your golden apple
breasts are

How the gods
must have loved us!

For they encoded
the ecstasy
of Creation
into our bodies

Executive Meeting

Heads
bald, with
or without
eyeglasses

Egg or apple
shaped
with or
without
facial hair

amuse me.

I see no
reflections
of the
divine
but selfish,
well groomed
brains

Feelings
(for an engagement)

It’s snowing in my heart
the most beautiful flake
what you are

In flowering spring
creek from sun melt snowflakes
what you are

This is your day,
drink it!
Sweet as
Bull’s Blood of
Eger *

Shades of red
subliminal passion
of Desire:
for something else
one day it might become!

Henceforth
I wish you life
live, love, cry
for each other

Do as you wish,
but never lie.

** Red wine from Eger, Hungary*

Grasshopper Man

The
insect woman
has loved,

now
she is ready
to devour you.

Do not
assume
the posture of
Death

Greek Love

I adore you

You are a rainbow petal
of an all-female
earth flower
throwing your scent
semi-wantingly
into the all-phallus wind
who is I
crazy
not really

just awake
with blood pulsating
all over my
beautiful body

In time *immemorial*
I was a flesh and
and blood fairy-poetess,
too
on the island of
Lesbos,
where I loved you once

When such
divine mysteries
were sacred
and sexually holy

Haiku in Prison

I.

Rocks of life
are suppressing me
yet
in sudden,
unanticipated
moments
gaps open
to write
a poem

II.

Rough people
scare me
yet I take delight
in their
simplicity

III.

Disguised like
a prisoner
in shackles
sin seems
harmless
as it
flows by

Haiku
in prison

Hail the Filipinos!

The arch
of their women's
eyebrows
are ambassadors
of heavenly
pleasures

On Sundays their
Catholic churches
are full
they don't know
any better, still
isn't it wonderful?

A tourist
saw them
using a
Willy Jeep's
engine to pump
water to their fields
then
merrily driving
into the sunset

The
survival
of the fittest

A nation
of hard working
nurses

If it weren't for
Imelda Marcos and her
two hundred pair
of shoes:

I would say
these are God's people,
the nicest!

Hemingway

Inundated
with shadow- thoughts
the Great Writer's
world darkened
'till just a simple act:
the trigger-pulling remained

He
ignored the Sun
the singing birds
the fleeing moment
pregnant with
eternity
what a stupidly missed
opportunity

But alas!

He reinforced
the divine right
to self-destruct
acquired in
the Garden of
Eden

This grove
now is littered
with skulls,
abandoned
except
the laughing Snake
and the terrified
Woman
under the Tree

Her

Woman!

The eternally
returning question

She made me
insane once
I almost suffocated
in her calculated
graces

Then I've been told
that she is
from Venus

So am I!
said I
realizing
the unfairness
of this statement
to my gender
in my logic-ridden
man-dog mind

Ever since
she is mine
when I
so desire

Hollywood Boulevard and Me

Morning,
dirty stars

Littered, urinated
streets
scattered neon lights

Colorful
shades penetrated
my opening
trembling
liver

Later,
I undressed
a blonde
in a dirty,
poorly lit
flooded motel room

on Hollywood Boulevard

I found

a rock
named Elsie
(by me)

She
waited for
a hundred thousand
years

Trampled upon
by dinosaurs

Seen a million
sunsets
after being
regurgitated
from the depths
of Earth

Then
we met.

I touched Her.

Sexual
sensations of
ages immemorial
vibrated within me,
and so indefinitely
more

How
could I tell
the feeling of
Michelangelo's
Adam, as he
materialized
into existence
from the
fingertip
of the
Father of
Heavens?

Introversion

Spare me not.
I am unfit.

A fatally ill
child of
a fallen star
and the devil
of a dark pit

Light years will
absolve me

Nothing else,
nothing

Involuntary Inclination

The press
presses and
taxes choking us
we unwind
for an hour
during
happy hour

Our human ties are
so ordinary
like a preordained priest's
predictable prayers
and his rosary

World powers
are using us
to inflict war wounds
on people
on other continents

The money men hidden
their true intentions
in commercials
which we recite
like first graders

The angels are
in tears,
regretting
ever making
love to
the apes

Our
un-Shakespearean,
pathetic end
inevitably
unfolds
as written

We run.

Into each other,
to Christ, Vishnu
sex and
alcohol

and so on,

trying
to find ourselves
hopelessly
in distractions

I, the Son of Horus
(the Lunatic)

I am
an incarnated Sphinx
with clipped wings
now
I must roll over
the dead bodies
of my evil deeds or
swim the river Styx

The Galactic Whore's
donut breasts and
her fly-catcher soul
earth-bounded me

am I a fly?

I can no more cry.
Why can't I
like vulnerable souls
no more cry?

The Dollar-God has killed me.
My hardened, dried blood
is food for pedestrian ants

Do you like the animals?
Honk if yes, otherwise
get lost, barbarian, say I
a proud member of the
Save The Whales Society

A homeless just wanted a quarter
away with you, man!
I stand for justice for all
and equality!

Jupiter and the Belly Dancer

In memory of Kim

Drums
and rattlers
harps and single-stringed
exotic violins are
whipping the blood
of the audience
and the dancer
making her
sweating sweet scent
transforming her limbs
into erotic, rhythmic snakes
her golden apple breasts
and mesmerizing nipples
are intoxicating
unseen but madly assumed
between her legs
the fountain of life
sacred to all men
are all fusing into
an irresistible power
of a goddess in flesh
the Universe
have chosen her
she is being fornicated
by the supreme and utmost
seducer himself

Jupiter

Love,

when
abused
is cheating
on Creation

Love is death:
this duality,
Yin and Yang
form Eternity

the Love of
man and woman
make up the Human
in bed and
in Society

Love keeps the
planets in orbit
the blood pulsating
in the heart

Ah, the heart!
a pile of
muscles, yet
so indefinitely
more
like the phallus

Love and lust
put the smile
on the cherry-lips
of women

Mad Dog

*In memory of an unarmed man**

Red on white
explicit the blood on the fangs
the belly swollen, screaming
the Mad Dog is charging!

Guilty are the ones
who did not embrace him
when the time was there
to love, for love

Eye for an eye
the Law is now
the guts, the blood
Nature is talking!

No more masters
or beggar's bones
those times passed
the Mad Dog is charging!

Stepping aside
once fearless owners
bribing the sniper-bullet
to do the dirty job

The wild, straight Intention died!
Crooked ways of the world
Prevail
Still
Will
Kill

Do you even know
what is love?
As you step over
a half man, half dog body
with a hole
between the eyes

* *He hijacked a school bus in Florida, in an attempt to force the Internal Revenue Service to talk to him about his financial distress, but was shot to death.*

Middle-East Childhood 2003

Not fairies
but planes
multiply
(with their bombs
above Ali Baba's magic castle)
in the darkness
of the Iraqi sky

Blood, oil and unholy water
desecrate
the blessed playground

Redemption will be
long and hard

Milky Hopes Fulfilled

I.
The cow has arrived.

Worry not
about milk now

II.
STARBUCKS!
says a friend as
where to meet

Great! say I
knowing my latte
has been taken care of

by corporate America
and the Cow

Monastery in Spain

As
bells toll,
the saga of a young monk
pure and devout
unfolds

Overcoming all
his erections,
he conquered
the Goddess
of Love

and the Devil
in the flesh

Mother

I
cry

I wanted
to love her
and hide my face
in her apron

For years
compulsively
and in random
I got slapped
by her
without reason

She
thought
the world was good
and without
her knowing
punished me
for the world
and father
not playing
along

Here I am
the tears
had frozen
on my cheeks
for years

Here I am
motherless
miserable
and beautiful

When soldiers die
they cry *mother*

What will be my cry
when I die?

Musical Isaiah

Mediocrity
is murderous.

Oh Lord,
be merciful
to my senses!

Deliver me from the
conveyor-belt culture
of our ages
of mechanized apes
the riders of
bad-tasting
pseudo-art waves

Save me
from people
without a true song
in their hearts
I pray!

Make my
ears deaf to songs
without birds
and flowers!

Life without
songs of true joy
would be a
slow damnation
to the followers
of the Almighty,

to the dwellers
of Taos

and
to Orpheus

Negative Solitude

Alone,
again

Nothingness
embraces me,
no pain.

All my burdens
nonexistent now

Benevolent
fog of the lonely,
cigarette smoke
engulfs me
as
I lay down
the thousandth
time,
cursing

nothing.

Negative Catharsis
(the Vision)

Six thousand
crabs are staring at me.

I try to leave, sideways

Step after step,
falling and getting up
again

The sounds of the Swamp
are drumming in my ears

the Broken Window
(an Indian chief in a forgotten
Western)
cracks open, and Voilà!
There are horses
drawn on all over the walls!

I try
to embrace my own heart,
crying

Too late!

Dropping the worthless flesh
I am catapulting
to the endless void

knocking my head
into a passing
asteroid

One Man

King?
Wake up!

Lord?
Kid me not!

Savior?
Get lost.

Just a man,
breaking bread
or
breathing heavily,
perspiring
under the arms
as rolling tables
madly in the
Temple

Then
the ultimate
sacrifice

Coming back on the
Third Day
was nothing,
but an act of

love,
unconditional

divine
that is

Perfection

Swallows singing
in misty morning
the ode of joy

Bullets singing
the song of death
far, far away
in war
and next door

Sky, wind
sweet grass
all spoke
to the Indians

There is
harmony

Included, but
not limited to:
the last cry of Bambi
between the jaws
of the Big Bad Wolf

Men butcher men
that is in order
as well

All incorporated
into the all-forgiving
Universe

Prayer

Dear Father,

whom we seek
but can't find
in Heaven,
may you show me
how to
be able eat
and create,
love and
embrace
without selling
my time

How not to
shed blood,
real or otherwise

Help me
not to rebel against
your hard hands
and understand
your bloody
sacrifice

I reckon
between You
and I
is me

how much more
complicated
could it be?

Prison

fake
laughter

skeletons
suppressed

murderers
and
pedophiles

winged shadows
filling the air

Question
(to a lover)

Are you
me?

My missing part?
You know,
I need
your soul,
the
beautifully-colored
jungle birds
in your mind

Your arms
your smile
the daily bath in your eyes
the all-feminine
you I need

My spirit aches
and afraid of you

Tell:
are you

me?

Reflections in the Forest

Deers
are jumping
with tears,
defenseless.
Gunshots.

Sunshine
and Death are
filling the
birdless air

as,
having
no choice
the Sky
(like a loving relative
at a funeral),
begins to cry

Ants ignoring
my ecstasy,
as the female
under me
steals my sobriety

Born to live
born to procreate
being a gear
in the great machinery

Who am I?
Fear not:
it is a good day
to die.

Seaman Leaving Port
(the loser)

Farewell
my lady of crazy,
naked nights
unparalleled

Curse me not
as
I can't give
it all: the keel
of my boat
strangely
has the will of
its own

The waves are
calling me
(again)

For this,
for Neptun's sake
please, bitte, perfavor!
understand
and forgive
me
as I climb
into other beds
thinking
I found
freedom
between a pair of
other legs,

Ahoy!

Self Analysis
(on an impulse)

I am
a minority
a crazy Hungarian
and a poet
occasionally

I cry of happiness
and sing with
a defiant heart
when sadness
clouds over me

I am
the dancer and
the musician
the needle
and the thread

I killed
emotions in others
and was
de-loved
promptly

nowadays,
I try
not to cause
calamity

I truly
loved women
they all taught me
one thing
like to King Solomon
that
all things
besides the love
of the Divine

(whatever you
imagine It to be)

are vanity

Seven Commandments
(inspired by the movie
"The Photographer")

let
an ancient
but living urge
to take you off
from the treadmill
of repeatedness
dictated by
your needs
and others

let
improvise
your next move

let
your bare feet
touch the grass

let
people
who just
surfaced
to interfere
with
your secular
existence

let
them touch
your life
you've been
brought together
for the occasion
by the unknown
and unpredictable
Designer
who has the
secret key to your
innermost desires

let
the stubborn child
quiet down in you

let
yourself
to be

Strange Couple

No silence,
just nothing.

Time is
on bypass
as falling snow
softly surrounds us

A pianist
somewhere
plays Chopin

the tone
gradually loses
its breath
just like
a fugitive slave
who is slowly
bleeding to death

Bells toll
from a distance

We leave.

Fog embraces us
as our steps echoing
in the dark street

We separate,
saying nothing

Surreal
(the frozen microsecond)

Lovely mannequins
stand still
making stiff
dance-like moves:
the ritual
of the dead

The moon, sinking among
obscure clouds
calls for her sister,
Europa
the beautiful
in vain

Then, suddenly
like in a microchip,
a malfunction:
God did not blink
when the unsuspecting
angels expected
(as the unexpecting
devils suspected)

now this reluctance
is holy,
part of history
perfect, like an
excited but
unfulfilled
woman's
burning desire
for the phallus
which might
catapult her

into temporary
tranquility

The Taj Mahal's Queen

in my head
is unreal

was the builder-king's
queen divine
or just a deluxe female
overall?

The Atheist's Prayer

I
was
illuminated

I knelt
next to the bed
and heard
my voice

Give us
our daily bread

without reservation
or else
we disintegrate
in the process
of obtaining it
and
the broken fragments
of our identities
will gravitate
towards hell

two fish
and some bread
is all we asking for,
nothing else

Amen.

The Beekeeper
(the New World Order)

You are so unique
and so special!
And so individual!

You fly whenever,
wherever you want!
You are so free!

Said the Beekeeper
to the Bee

The Bird Man and His Shadow
(Navajo Indian reservation, Arizona)

Mount the horse,
good Navajo brother!

The ride ends
as the Sun sets
where the Sacred Fire
(this ancient time machine)
awaits us

Let us see, we pray
and lo!
Dancing in the flames
the forefathers' spirits
iron birds and
burning arrows
and the Roadman*
is mourning
for the orphaned Dineh*

Flowers of your blood
are cut, laid in mud
Under the dollar-god
life is but
a Coke-flavored dream
the Spirit is broken
our women and Mother Earth
hear me, oh my brother,
are desecrated!

The Bird Man visits
no more!
Our tepees lost
their magic circle

Mount the horse,
good Navajo brother!

In our souls
shall unfold
the face of
the Creator
to bless
and give It
to our sons
to inherit

Yateh! *

**Roadman - spiritual leader*
**Dineh - people*
**Yateh: - greeting, well-wishing*

The Cat and the Mice

(In memory of a
Jewish-Hungarian journalist)

I
tried
to make
them stronger, to have fun
by playing catch-and-run
but in their
pitiful pettiness
and uncreativeness
they kept hiding from me,
life and themselves

To
relieve
the poor creatures
from their deprived fates
I, the Cat
lovingly ate them

So
they hired
government dogs
with guns and uniforms

A bad day
for me, but
a holiday for them:
all the mice came
out from hiding, lined up
clapping, tapping, whistling
as I
stood by
strong in Spirit
witnessing my own Death

Oh, these little grey people!
Wrong again!

I, the Cat
unbeknownst to them
have eight more lives
to teach, love, play
and to eat them

The Derelict and Gauguin

This room is
a nice room
with plush walls
and no sharp
objects in it

The mirror
reflects
my unshaven face
the people are nice
smiling, wearing white
and ready to jump

The TV is on,
elections.
Jobs! Jobs!
We need more jobs!
thunders the
President,
the Candidate
and the Mob

Funny men!
the cancer is
in their hearts
yet all the talking
is about
the stomach

My doctors
mimicking healing
with their pills

One day
I just might
trick them!
and will run away
to Tahiti
to paint with

Gauguin

The Derelict King

Once ruled
vast land and riches

now wearing the
(executed)
court-jester's cap
the king,
without any
kingish features
sets out
to no-man's land
to locate
his kingdom
Unreal

A bad copy
of king Lear

The Knight's Ghost

I am
bound
by her love

She
flashed
her golden hair
and waved
farewell gently
before fading
into eternity

I saw
her velvet
body again
her nipples were
kissed by
sensual,
loving water
when she swam
with fairies
in the magic lake
of timeless
passion

a sight
so charged
with feminity
unbearable for a man
with or without
a body

Midnight come.

I am drawn
to the Vortex
let the walls
of this old
haunted fort
collapse

Eternity is but
a colorless painting
without her graces

The Party

Dry
smiles,
plenty the
food

to look @ that woman
makes me feel
ordinary
so
I try
to picture her
naked

Loud
speakers dumping
noise-mud on our
human ties

Drink, drink
drunken

I loved you so much!

Now?
I wish your non-existence
woman of measures
and
compressed sexual desires

assumed your
handicapped
god
allows

Shine off,
shine off

Spit.
Smile.
Be nice.
Nod
to stupid statements

Leave.

The Policeman's Ballad

The
lead wasp
sings her deadly song
as she's
passing
by my ear
at two-thousand
feet per second

I think of mother
and
wonder if
survival is
a sin

The man
reloads his gun
behind the wall

There is
no time left to think
for him or for me

but to kill

The Virgin’s Monologue

I think
I am aroused!

Oh my!
What am I
to do
or not to do
now?

Curiosity
(what is sex?
Is it like in the
movies?)
and
trembling love
devours me

I am
a woman to be
by ancient and
unwritten law
I am sacred

Shall I let him
the one
who unearthed
the hot lava under
my anxious volcano
to embrace
and love me
naked?

Oh dear!

I already know
of his longings
and what's he's
unsure of

a female advantage
since the dawn
of the Ages

The Woman

The eternal Female
madly mourns her
loved mate:

her distorted,
carnivorous face
reflects in the
male blood
shed by her
very own hand
as
with one charming,
natural
yet feminine move
she takes
the hairpin from the
beloved mans's heart
and graciously resets it
in her golden hair
then,
with ever lively
self evident curiosity,
she surveys the
near-by herd of
qualified Man-Bulls,
in search for
of an another male
to fulfill her mysterious
contract with the
Mother of All Fertility
(a timeless duty)

The mystery of
life and death,
oh man
is rather simple matter
compared to
Woman, your
inevitable destiny

the Holy Virgin
and the
vicious Harlot,
both in one body:
bow to her
majestic duality!

Want more madness?

Add her third,
and most
sacred role:

Maternity

Trilogy

I.

Deliver me
from the path
of my
own aimless
imagination

II.

I dreamt of
roles, perhaps
heroic
they laid a trap
to my soul

III.

If you hurt me
you kill me
and
kill yourself
inside of
me

Two Questions
(to a man from Texas)

I.

Who
told you
to cast the die
for the destiny
of the planet,
and for the future
of our children's
children
without knowing
Creation?

II.

Are you,
who's warships
destroy places
of worship
a sheep
in your Church
for the reason
of ignorance,
lack of
conscience
or for
the fake sense of
absolution?

I wonder

Unblessed Union

They lied
before the priest

Who himself
was not sure
what love
really meant

the
Ruler
of the sky
just nodded
by hearing
his name used

Hindus
they were
not

nevertheless
the consequences
of their selfish
actions have
resonated
for Ages

Vision

Cube up!
Said a Multi-Dimensional,
Multi-Corporational
Global-Capital
and International
human-looking thing
to me

Earth is a cube!
Said an another
strange creature
in suit and tie
proudly looking
right angled
himself

I felt an urge to look
at the sky
and lo and behold!
It sure seemed
somewhat square

Alarmed
I scratched my head
but, thank Goodness
this good old skull of mine
was still curved and round
as always,
like the Planets
the women's shapely
rear or their beautiful
frontal weaponry
those sweet melons
or any other
blessed fruits
under the Sky

What a relief!
The Creator
did not artificate
his creations!

Or my mind.

Want

Shameless
skyscrapers
wedding cakes
three feet high
jetplanes with
nuclear bombs
bankers with
cell phones

alienate me.

Megalomania
à la carte
peripherally
contaminates
my intimate
relationship
with reality

I am tired of
magazines
and plastic,
skinny models

I need
a real woman
with true eyes,
real scent and
frontal apples

I am tired of
this virtual reality
saturating our life

I am tired of
this Nintendo-age
of pseudo-pleasures

I want
blood in my veins
and
the handshake
of the Almighty,
who will
hopefully
let me in
on the
secret

Why?

War People

War is
war.

For the last
five thousand years
nothing really
differs

Here, there
against, for,
or instigated
by the U.S.
or us

Races against racists
or vice versa
by whatever means:
bayonet, bullet, bomb
napalm, mines and
agent orange;
last but not least:
the blessing of a
nuclear holocaust

Once we sent there,
we kill the Japs
the Krauts
or the Viet Kong
notwithstanding
the damn Iraqis
with half a ration
in their Muslim
stomachs

You name it
we do what we must
The mystery of
Good and Evil
shall be left
to solve
(in lack of a better name)

to God, who
blesses America and
(would you ever guessed?)
any other country
under the Sky

Watchman In the Tower
(the prison guard)

Midnight
descended
on his shoulders

misplaced
again
he whispered
to himself
or rather into the night
of a thousand
loneliness

then,
bit by bit
he reinvented
the subatomic
particles of
time and space
in his own
brain cells
to prolong his life
one more
sunrise

Two crows,
black as
moonless sky
landed on his
shoulders

harbingers
of Death

Without a Woman

The holy
redemption
of the vulva
has been denied,
and the Mother of
All Desires suspended me
for waking up uncalled
the latent, all-giving female
in her daughters, hibernating
mysteriously in the magic triangle
(Bermuda, that is)
and for tasting madly
those two sweet melons

But is it not what they
longed for all along?

A man is a man;
to fight, to toil
and to bleed
to Earth
He was born

To bear this
unbearable Life
for his Woman
and his Child
He shall die
if He must

Hear ye,
Female Universe!
In exchange,
all he's asking
is an Embrace:
give it with
an open heart,

or do not
give at all!

About the Author
by himself

I was born the second of three sons in 1959 to Iren and Ferenc Katona, both of whom were teachers. At fourteen I began writing poems, mostly as a compensatory activity in response to the overwhelming input received from my environment and the distorted human relations I had witnessed and was a part of. Feeling wary of the Communist regime, I fled Hungary in 1979. My defection and the time I spent in an Italian refugee camp proved defining experiences for the rest of my life.

I moved to Chicago where I remained mostly unemployed. With my last two hundred dollars I purchased a one-way ticket to Los Angeles based on a rumor circulated among my fellow Hungarian immigrants that "In California the sun always shines, it never rains and every apartment building must have a swimming pool by law."

In Los Angeles, I practiced several highly esteemed vocations such as a busboy, janitor, bouncer, cabdriver, plumber, glass man, and for one night, car re-possessor (I decided however, that getting shot at was not worth the pay). Eventually I founded a medium-sized construction company of my own, folk-dancing, drinking and writing on the side.

I also became interested in acting, and auditioned for several studios. I found all but one director to be lacking in their conception of true art. Only Rene, the Frenchman from the Open Fist self-funded theater impressed me with his artistic understanding. I became a member of this theater after an audition in which I recited one of my poems (in my native Hungarian tongue) and portrayed a drunkard. In the end this wonderful enterprise closed its doors. The artificial and glamour-oriented Hollywood art scene seems to reject any genuine artistic endeavour that is alien to its own nature.

I am only now beginning to publish my poems for a variety reasons, including the advice from Andras Fodor, a writer who lives in Transylvania [formerly a Hungarian territory, now Romania]: *"Write only, when you absolutely have no other alternative"*.

My future plans include becoming involved with film and theater as both a writer and director. I have a ten-year old daughter, Réka, named after the wife of Attila, the Hun.

About the Book

Poems are like stones.

You can admire them uncut, or sculpt them into the dreams of your illuminated nights. Like stones, poems can also be weapons, too. There are precious stones and precious poems; poems which love to attach themselves to the velvet skin of women. Poems can be like building stones, cast aside or being made into a shrine.

Paul Katona, a native of Hungary shares the sacred gems of his altar with you, and also shows you the stone ax with which he uses to combat his own demons. He invites you too, into his secret garden filled with statues of Greek goddesses, allowing you a glimpse into the depth of the female mystery, cruelty, beauty and sensuality.

He cannot share selectively, but give himself in his entirety. To complete this communion however, you must make a decision to become open, too. Ready? Say yes! And welcome this compassionate, cynical, touching, and challenging world of his collection into your life.

You will emerge with magic, never seen precious stones - they will beautify your world, and will open new doors of perceptions. Some of his poems will appear politically motivated, but closer inspection will reveal that the underlying impetus, as always - is the human condition itself, a condition constantly threatened by various political, commercial, or even religious, establishments. The author's *Ars Poetica* maintains that there exists no subject that can not be written about in a poem.

The capability to recognize, transmute, and integrate any phenomenon into the sacred is the true litmus test of an artist and the decisive question of the artist remains: on what part of the spectrum at any given moment, are we? The world is all inclusive *and* indefinite in the same time. Poetry, like music, is a sacred language, a higher form of expression. Get ready to remove the dust guards from your own mirror, and rediscover yourself in this sometimes graphic, defining and romantic realm, *The Bird Man and His Shadow*.

www.ingramcontent.com/pod-product-compliance
Ingram Content Group UK Ltd.
Pitfield, Milton Keynes, MK11 3LW, UK
UKHW041847190726
13854UKWH00002B/754

9 781412 036429